Millennials
Incorporated

Millennials Incorporated

The Big Business of Recruiting,
Managing and Retaining
the World's New Generation of
Young Professionals

❖

LISA ORRELL
Speaker ❖ Author ❖ Consultant

Intelligent Women Publishing
A Wyatt-MacKenzie Imprint

Millennials Incorporated
The Big Business of Recruiting, Managing and
Retaining the World's New Generation
of Young Professionals

SECOND EDITION

ISBN: 978-1-932279-82-5

Library of Congress Control Number: 2007939624

  Robert Half International

Intelligent Women Publishing
A Wyatt-MacKenzie Imprint

Imprint information: www.WyMacPublishing.com

Printed in the United States of America

Dedication

This book is dedicated to the Millennial Professionals on my personal business team and to the ones who are now my business colleagues in the professional world. It's also dedicated to my family team: Adrienne, Jenner, Julie, Ruby, Ma & Pa Jones, Mom, and Papa O.

TABLE OF CONTENTS

What Other Professionals Are Saying...   9

INTRODUCTION
Why Are Millennial Professionals Such a Hot Commodity? 13

❖

PART ONE
Understanding the Millennial Professionals

Chapter 1: How Millennial Professionals Came To Be: 21
Background of (Common) Childhood
Environments

Chapter 2: Millennial Education and Multi-Cultural   25
Upbringing

Chapter 3: Millennial Views on Parents, Family, and Sex 29

Chapter 4: Millennial Thoughts on Community Service,   33
Diversity, and Politics

Chapter 5: The Relationship between Millennial Chicks   37
& Millennial Guys

Chapter 6: A Snapshot of Differences between Millennial, 41
GenX, & Boomer Professionals

Chapter 7: Key Millennial Traits All Employers Need to Know 45

❖

PART TWO
Attracting, Recruiting & Retaining Millennial Professionals

Chapter 8: Innovative Ideas for *Attracting* Millennial   53
Professionals

Chapter 9: Hot Buttons for *Recruiting* Millennial   59
Professionals

Chapter 10: Unique Strategies for *Retaining* Millennial 65
Professionals

PART THREE
Managing & Motivating Millennial Professionals

Chapter 11: Common Complaints Managers Have About   73
Millennial Professionals

Chapter 12: Solid Strategies for *Managing* Millennial   79
Professionals

Chapter 13: Sound Solutions for *Motivating* Millennial   87
Professionals...and a Handful of Guaranteed
Motivation Busters!

❖

PART FOUR
A Global Perspective & Two Bonus Chapters

Chapter 14: A Global Perspective: Are Millennials the   97
Same Around the World?

BONUS
Chapter 15: Success Defined: What Gen Y Wants in   101
a Career, *courtesy of Yahoo! HotJobs and
Robert Half International*

BONUS
Chapter 16: The Key ABC's of Employee Engagement,   113
*courtesy of the Employee Engagement
Network*

❖

PART FIVE
It's All About Lisa

Chapter 17: Specific Ways Lisa Can Benefit Your   127
Company

About the Author: Lisa Orrell   131

What Other Professionals Are Saying About Lisa's Book & Presentations

❖

"I LOVE YOUR BOOK! I just bought 7 more copies to pass around to my education team. With over 10,000 students (mostly Millennials) who sign up for my 100-plus schools every year, I am always looking for brilliant information that can help me to understand them better. Your book is right on the mark!"

W. Claybaugh, Dean & Co-Founder of Paul Mitchell Schools
& Author of BE NICE (OR ELSE!)

"Even down here in Australia we've come across Lisa Orrell and her world-class analysis of the Millennials. As leading social researchers analyzing generational trends across Asia, I can tell you that the issues addressed in **Millennials Incorporated** are indeed global challenges. Lisa speaks with authority on these emerging employees and she offers excellent insights into this global generation."

Mark McCrindle, Social Researcher, www.mccrindleresearch.com

"Everyone loved you! There is so much excitement and ideas surfacing since your presentations. In addition, you have such engaging style that it feels like I've known you forever!"

E. Wainwright, Blue Cross/Blue Shield of Michigan, Vice President
of Workforce Diversity & Inclusion

"My responsibility is to recruit new college grads for our company. Our CEO has made that a priority in our recruiting efforts over the next 3 years. So not only did I find Lisa's book extremely helpful for insight into this new generation, but we also hired her for all 3 of her seminars and our Boomer and Gen X Managers have found them to be very helpful. Not only do I recommend her book, but hiring her to speak at your company, too."

> Evelyn M., Manager of University Learning & Development
> at large technology company

"This book is the best resource I have seen on how to communicate, hire and retain the new generation of young professionals. I've bought quite a few copies to share with clients and colleagues!

Everyone is talking about the generational differences, but Lisa Orrell has done the research and has come up with practical, easy to implement solutions on how to effectively communicate and motivate this generation and how those of us from different generations (especially the baby boomers) can learn from them as well. This book is well written and should be a handbook for anyone involved in the recruitment of personnel and for anyone who manages people. As an HR professional, I found the book not only educational (lots of aha moments!) yet really fun to read."

> J. Prescott, HR Professional & Executive Recruiter
> for 25 years

"I am attaching a letter of request to invite you to speak at the Professional Business Women of California Sacramento Conference. You were one of the **most memorable and motivating speakers** at PBWC's San Francisco Conference this year (attendance was over 6000!) and we would like you to please consider speaking in Sacramento. You really were awesome!"

> Cathy D., Associate Event Producer

"Lisa's book is a must read for any company that is committed to building an inclusive culture and tapping into the potential and talent of the Millennial generation. Her practical tips, ideas and strategies address what we 'perceive' to be barriers in working with Millennials and are helpful in bringing us to the "reality" of working together inclusively! Lisa has captured the essence of information we need to know "now" to bridge the gaps with working with a multi-generational workforce."

> Lisa A. Clayton, President Source Potential, Inc.,
> www.sourcepotential.com

"This is a great book to help understand the new generation, what makes them tick and how to manage them. This is the kind of information that a VP of Human Resources would love and I've already recommended this to several HR executives to help them with current recruitment efforts! Also very informative for marketers who need to understand this generation—working with them, recruiting them and marketing to them!"

> Sherry Prescott-Willis, Marketing Expert, Author of *Market This!*
> www.Market-This.org

"As a Senior Hiring Manager for a well-known company, filling open positions has become a major challenge because the competition for the right talent is so fierce in the Bay Area. **Millennials Incorporated** gave me incredible insights into how this generation thinks, how they act and what they are looking for in employers and their careers. It didn't take long to read and I am pretty sure my job just got easier. Thank you, Lisa Orrell!"

> D. Dalton, Senior Hiring Manager at large corporation

"Wow!!!!!!!!!!! You were terrific.

It was great having you speak to our HR group last Thursday! Thank you so much for your time, energy, humor and talent to "tell it like it is." You came across with credibility, experience and knowledge—a winning combination.

The wisdom you shared was extremely helpful—there have been several emails going back and forth about your meaty information. Thank you again!"

C. Young, Senior Director, Leading Recruitment Agency

"Lisa Orrell is an expert in this breaking new field of generation relations…her seminars and book are resources that every innovative company needs!"

Rayona Sharpnack, Founder & CEO, Institute for Women's Leadership, www.womensleadership.com, Author *Trade Up: 5 Steps for Redesigning Your Leadership & Life from the Inside Out*

"As an expert on generational relationships myself, I can honestly say that Lisa's book provides valuable insights into the Millennials! Her book is a must-read for management teams and HR/Recruiting professionals."

Misti Burmeister, Author: *From Boomers to Bloggers: Success Strategies Across Generations*, www.inspirioninc.com

Note: Many of these testimonials are from people whose companies have strict policies prohibiting public endorsements and testimonials. Therefore, several peoples' names and company names needed to be withheld. However, Lisa can (privately) provide you with a complete Client Reference List, with contact info, should you require it.

INTRODUCTION

Why Are Millennial Professionals Such a Hot Commodity?

❖

Welcome to the Second Edition of my book! I've come across lots of new info that I wanted to share AND added two bonus chapters that were not in the First Edition. Plus, I added a new chapter answering the popular question, "Are Millennials the same around the world?" You may be surprised by the answer!

I've really enjoyed meeting so many people on this journey and really appreciate all of the positive feedback I have gotten on my book. So, without further delay, let's get started.

As you read this, Millennial Professionals are being actively recruited prior to, and upon, college graduation. Some are already busy navigating the waters of their first professional job since being hired a year or so ago.

And as I write this, companies are hiring me to conduct seminars to educate their HR executives and internal recruiters about attracting and recruiting Millennial Professionals, as well as conduct seminars to educate their GenX and Boomer employees about managing, motivating and retaining them. So, this isn't just me saying they are a big deal to the future of our professional workforce; companies all over the U.S. and abroad are starting to see it, too.

Why has this new generation of young professionals turned into such a hot commodity and now covered all over the media? One key factor is the looming reality of the *Boomer Brain Drain* that companies across the country are going to feel over the next 20 years (starting now as the oldest Boomers hit retirement age). Here's one simple statistic, out of many, from the Office of Employment Projections that will quickly put this into perspective: *The average large company in the U.S. will lose 30-40% of its workforce due to retirement over the next 5-10 years.* Ouch.

We have as many GenXers on the planet as there is going to be, so the replacements for this massive Boomer exodus are the Millennial Professionals. That is why M.B.A. students are being offered amazing employment packages, starting salaries are being jacked-up higher than ever, and impressive signing bonuses are being offered. These young adults are currently being pursued and courted like top college draft picks entering the NBA. *Basically, recruiting and retaining them has turned into a big, competitive business.*

And I'd like to point out that quite a few books have been written about Millennials and the multi-generational workforce. However, most of them were written quite some time ago (mainly between 1997-2003) before the first wave of Millennial Professionals really started to even graduate from college; even before many of the oldest Millennials had graduated from high school; and even before demographers really knew what to call them (Gen Y? N-Gens? Echo Boomers? Oh-Ohs?).

We now know, through recent research, that a majority of this generation prefer to be called the Millennial Generation, and most demographers agree their generation's official "start date" is 1982 and ends around 2002.

The first Millennial class *officially* said to graduate high school was the Class of 2000. And since the average college student now takes 5-7 years to graduate with a Bachelor's or Master's degree, this generation is just NOW starting to enter and impact professional work environments.

I admire the authors who got a jump on writing about Millennials and discussing them as employees, however (if you agree with the 1982 start date) back in the late 1990s the oldest Millennials were about 15 years old. I doubt many of you seeking new *professional* talent back then were actively hiring teenagers for those positions, so you probably weren't reading books about them. And most of those books were about hiring and managing Millennials in "teen" type jobs like retail, fast food restaurants, and casual dining eateries.

But guess what? Those teenagers have grown-up and the Millennial Professionals have arrived. So *Millennials Incorporated* is targeted at employers, of any size, wanting to recruit and retain these young adults to be their next generation of managers, executives, and leaders in professional work environments NOW. And this book provides current info about what they expect from their employers NOW.

I don't plan on covering much about "how the generations can all work together in harmony." My primary goal is to tell you all about the Millennial Professionals *as people*, and then explain how you can effectively adjust your recruitment strategies and (possibly) your GenX or Boomer management style to best work with them. There are well-known companies currently spending millions of dollars to up-date their recruiting efforts, corporate cultures, and management styles to accommodate this unique generation so you should probably keep reading. Again, recruiting and retaining them has become a *big* business.

Through my research I also realized many GenX and Boomer professionals in today's business world have no clue about this new generation entering their domain. What I do find is that most everyone I speak to shares the same overall perception of them: "They seem lazy, spoiled, self-centered, don't want to work hard, and need so much hand-holding. Oh, but they are really tech savvy."

All of this inspired me to write this book. *Are these personality traits and views accurate? If so, how on earth do you deal with them in a work environment?* After all, they are YOUR next generation of managers and executives! But don't panic, we'll get into more about this later.

In the meantime, here is another reason why I (and you) should care about Millennial Professionals: According to a *USA Today* article written in October of 2006, entitled "Gen Y Sits on Top of the Consumer Food Chain," there are an estimated 80 MILLION kids and young adults in this new generation.

And Neil Howe, generational expert and co-author of *Millennials Rising: The Next Great Generation*, personally told me that he predicts there will be closer to 100 million Millennials by the end of their collective lifetimes (once you add in immigrants in their age range that arrive to the U.S.). This makes them the biggest generation in the history of our country! Yes, even bigger than the Boomers.

Our country (and world!) has just begun to feel their impact as they reach their mid-20s. And, as with generations in the past, this generation will create new definitions for: Work environments, success, leadership, communication, management, entrepreneurship, corporate culture, and professional relationships.

So keep reading...*you can't effectively attract, recruit, manage, and retain them if you don't really know them!*

P.S. I started a blog since I wrote the First Edition! I keep it current with great tips for managers and execs from ANY department and from companies of ANY size. Human Resource, Recruitment and Diversity professionals also get a lot from it:

Check it out: http://blog.generationrelations.com/

PART ONE

Understanding the Millennial Professionals

❖

"The young do not know enough to be prudent,
and therefore they attempt the impossible,
and achieve it, generation after generation."

Pearl S. Buck, award-winning author and first woman
to win both the Nobel and Pulitzer Prizes

C H A P T E R   O N E

How Millennial Professionals Came To Be: Background of (Common) Childhood Environments

❖

Here is some perspective to chew on: The Millennial Professionals graduating from college are members of the generation of kids raised with "Baby On Board" signs stuck to their parents' minivan window; using car seats and bike helmets were required when they were children; and when they were reaching puberty every state implemented some sort of driver's license law requiring additional "practice hours," and/or created laws limiting the amount of teens in a car, and/or enforced driving curfews for teens.

My teen years were spent packing 10 friends in a car and party hopping until late at night. And when I was a young kid riding a bike, the only thing between my skull and the asphalt was my hair. *My point?* This generation has been raised with laws to <u>protect</u>

them more than any other generation in our history. Society, not just their parents, has been telling them they are "special and valued" since Day One.

Millennial Professionals are the sons and daughters of Boomers and older GenXers, and grandsons and granddaughters of older Boomers or Veterans. So it is pretty amazing how little the Boomers and GenXers, now the managers and executives in the workforce, know about Millennial Professionals.

The Millennials in general are also the first generation of kids in our history encouraged to talk openly about their feelings in public and at home. They were (and are) also encouraged to participate in family and household decisions at a much earlier age. "Children should be seen and not heard" was eliminated when the Millennial kids started arriving. Our country turned into a "pro kid" society when they were born, and this generation was immediately put on a pedestal, coddled, nurtured, and treated with respect by their Baby Boomer and GenX parents. Many were raised with Veteran generation grandparents, which have influenced them greatly in terms of manners and morality. We'll discuss more on that later.

The first wave of children born as Millennial Professionals (around 1982) hit their teens just as "angry" GenX bands like Pearl Jam and Nirvana became popular (I love those bands, but you have to admit they were a bit on the dark side), thus giving kids at the time a pop culture grunge branding for which most adults didn't care. The teens in the 90s were categorized as angry, clueless, non-caring, heavily into drugs, sloppy in style, lazy, etc. The teen girls from that period are now, however, the ones in college and graduating college, and are the ones excelling past the young men in academics (as you'll read later in this book).

Millennial parents encouraged family involvement from their kids early on, and as a result, many experts believe the average 10-year-old today is probably as mature and outspoken as the average 16-year-old was in the 1960s. Their parents respect their opinions and even seek their children's advice in purchasing decisions for the home and college selection.

And with regards to "protectiveness," recently a college official coined the term "helicopter parents." It refers to the fact that most Millennial Professionals have parents who are always hovering over them and are ultra protective. This generation has constantly had an active "team" around them for nurturing, encouragement, and success: 1-2 hands-on Boomer or GenX parents, Boomer or Veteran grandparents, teachers, guidance counselors, therapists, coaches, tutors, advisors, and local and federal government (through the "protection" laws I mentioned before).

Neil Howe, who I mentioned in the Introduction, co-author of *Millennial Rising: The Next Great Generation*, found that this generation tends to share seven core traits: "They are special, sheltered, confident, team-oriented, conventional, pressured, and achieving."

Does THAT sound like the sex crazed, substance abusing, teenagers the Boomer and GenX media execs continually show on television and in the movies? I don't think so.

C H A P T E R   T W O

Millennial Education & Multi-Cultural Upbringing

❖

The "spoiled" and "entitled" perception that much of society has of the Millennial Professionals is somewhat true. But their entitlement belief is not typically based on laziness and expecting things to just be handed to them. The Millennial Professionals tend to be very demanding (of themselves and others), and understand that it is their responsibility to work hard to get what they want. Out of the seven core traits that I mentioned before, *special, confident, and achieving* can often be misunderstood as *cocky, arrogant, and deserving.*

And test scores in high school and college entrance competition show the Millennial Professionals are smart and they work hard. Their sense of entitlement is based on wanting what they want, and working hard to get it. This is a generation of young adults that is highly competitive and worked hard in the classroom.

This is a group of kids and young adults that did well, and continues to do well, in school at all grade levels, and is rewarded in the classroom by teachers and peers, and at home by doting parents. This ambition and desire for "success and rewards" has been instilled in them from birth, with Boomer or GenX parents telling them they can do anything they put their minds to. This is a go-getter generation!

In 2007, New Media, in association with Bendixen & Associates, conducted an in-depth survey of 600 Millennials in California ranging in age from 16 to 22. The end result was a Special Report called *California Dreamers: A Public Opinion Portrait of the Most Diverse Generation the Nation Has Known.*

Two of the most important statistics from the survey that employers need to be aware of are these: 78% of Millennials said their lives would be better in 10 years, and an astounding 96% said this statement best describes their view of the future: *"If I work hard, I can achieve my goals."*

Again, does this seem like a generation of young adults that are lazy and clueless?

Another very important fact employers need to be aware of is that the Millennial Chicks are dominating college enrollment and blowing away their male colleagues in terms of grades. Also, colleges ranging from Ivy League to state universities have recently seen the women in their graduating classes receive a majority of their highest academic honors. This means that all you GenX and Boomer bosses need to be keenly aware of this smart and powerful group of women entering the workforce. All recent statistics are showing that a majority of them are truly more qualified for the entry level jobs you have (in terms of grades and academic achievements) than the young men are.

As the mother of a young son, that was hard to say, but that is the reality of what's happening in colleges today, in the late-2000s.

If you want more details on this topic, I strongly recommend getting your hands on this *New York Times* article from July 6, 2006: "At Colleges, Women Are Leaving Men in the Dust."

I have permission from *The New York Times* to quote info from it in my *Chickonomics* book (due out in 2008), and some of the factoids are pretty amazing about how the Millennial Chicks are doing, and have been doing, the past five years or so in colleges across the country.

One other thing employers need to note about Millennial Chicks: They don't expect to have to "earn" a male colleague's respect because they are "women." Millennial Chicks were raised to believe they are equal to men, and will expect to be treated as such the minute they walk through your doors. These women will not hesitate to demand it if you don't offer it.

Another interesting fact about Millennial Professionals (both genders) is that they are part of the first truly multi-cultural generation. Don't you notice when you see a group of Millennial aged friends sitting in a mall or restaurant it oftentimes looks like a mini meeting at the United Nations? In the United States, one in three Millennial Professionals are not Caucasian. These kids are part of a more ethnically diverse population than any generation before them. And many of them have friends, and get into romantic relationships with people, whose ethnicity differs from their own. In the 2007 *California Dreamers* survey I mentioned earlier, 87% of respondents said they were fine with marrying or having a life partner of a different race.

They are also the first generation to be able to make friends with people all over the world via the Internet and lead a "global lifestyle" from their homes. These young adults have been communicating with other youth all over the world since their teens through community sites like MySpace and FaceBook. So traveling the world or choosing a career that requires international travel is not something that seems odd or out-of-reach to them. This means that many Millennial Professionals coming to you for a job will likely embrace travel and hope to land a position where international travel is offered.

C H A P T E R   T H R E E

An Overview of Millennial Values: Parents, Family, and Sex

❖

As I mentioned in the previous section, unlike the former GenX generation, Millennial Professionals are not shy about proclaiming close ties to, and respect for, their parents. While Boomers decried their parental authority figures and GenXers were cynical critics of the older generation(s), the Millennial Professionals like to spend time with their parents, and many consider their parents an integral part of their social circle.

I found that interesting since, on the flip side of this adoration, many Millennial Professionals express a loathing for the label of "Generation Y" because they do not want to be in the shadow of the previous generation. They see GenX as more self-centered and cynical than they are, and feel the title "Gen Y" simply makes them an extension of the one generation they relate to least of all before them.

We'll get into this more later, but suffice to say the potential clash between Millennial Professionals and GenXers in the workplace is more likely than between Millennial Professionals and Boomers (or Veterans still working).

Millennial Professionals do not try to conform, but instead prefer to express themselves in fashion, opinion, and community involvement. This is the generation raised with MTV's "Rock the Vote" and "Zero Tolerance." Statistics show messages like these, along with influence from their close parental relationships, have greatly influenced this generation's values. You have Boomer's joking that living with their kids is like having parents again…busting them for "bad" behavior (smoking, drinking, etc.).

Saying no to sex has increased due to the fact that they are much more aware of the dangers of STDs than prior generations, and they are a goal-oriented generation where accidentally getting pregnant doesn't fit into their long-term goals of college and career. Although there has been a lot of media attention put on their term for casual sex, known as "hooking up," it's really no more earth shattering than the "free love" mentality of the 1960s and 1970s, or the coke hazed promiscuity that was rampant with teens and young adults in the excessive 1980s.

Millennials possess a level of "old fashioned" morality reminiscent of the G.I. (aka: WWII or Veteran) Generation. This is very different from how teens were in the 70s and 80s. All statistics show that Millennials are choosing a very different path than their parents did when they were teens, and they seem to be highly focused on family values, personal respect, and following the rules (they have been raised in a society filled with rules just for them!).

So don't let the skimpy skirts, droopy pants, piercings and

tattoos fool you. Recent polls have shown that 2/3 of Millennial teens are actually offended (at some level) by the overt sex and vulgarity shown in the media today.

And this increasing tilt towards modesty is becoming more evident among the current Millennial Chick teenagers. Author Wendy Shalit recently published a book called "Girls Gone Mild" which discusses this new trend of girls and young women beginning to rebel against the wild, sexy behavior and fashions of this era's bad girls, such as Britney and Paris.

And there is an increase of new sites discussing and advocating more modest fashion for Millennial Chicks, such as ModestApparelUSA.com and ModestByDesign.com. As history has always shown, we're bound to have another wave of wild kids in another generation, but it looks like the Millennial teens coming up could be the ones bringing us back to more conservative fashion and milder behavior for awhile.

This also brings up an interesting point I'd like to share: Many experts predict we may even start seeing a more conservative wave of television programming, movies, and shifts in offensive lyrics in music, and in *styles* of music (coming back to more melodic music, with more romantic angles and easy-to-understand lyrics like that of the 70s), as the Millennial Professionals reach decision-making positions in media careers (replacing GenX and Boomers). It'll be interesting to see if that happens. We'll know soon since they are now in, and entering, the professional workforce!

C H A P T E R   F O U R

Millennial Thoughts on Community Service, Diversity, and Politics

❖

Millennial Professionals understand the value in helping others, their community, and the world. Did you know that around 50% of all Millennial Professionals volunteered for community service in high school? Many high schools actually require volunteering in the community to graduate. That wasn't even discussed when I was in school!

This belief in "helping others" is more prevalent than in prior generations, which is why Millennial Professionals tend to be highly aware of social injustice and more apt to think in terms of the "greater good." On average, a Millennial puts in more time than a middle-aged GenXer when it comes to community service. A recent poll revealed that 44% of them have participated in some community or charitable activity within the past twelve months, as compared to 35% of GenXers during the same time period.

I'm feeling really guilty right now.

Along this same vein, I saw actress and women's rights activist, Marlo Thomas, interview a group of Millennial Chicks who were all 25-years-old, and had just graduated college. This was for her series called "In Search of the Modern Woman" that aired on *The Today Show* in May of 2007. She asked them their opinions of celebs like Britney Spears, Lindsay Lohan, and Paris Hilton. Contrary to popular belief, all of these young women said they thought these young celebs seemed "lost" and they stated that they certainly didn't idolize them. When asked whom they did respect and look up to, they listed people such as: Their parents, Oprah, Bono, and Angelina Jolie (the three celebrities specifically for all they do for humanity).

We have all seen human-interest stories highlighting young kids and teens that launch regional and sometimes national fundraising activities to help those less fortunate. Indeed, the Millennial Professionals consider themselves *global citizens* and are concerned with the well being of others in the U.S. and abroad.

Basically, Millennial Professionals have been raised with a strong sense of community, and as a group, they focus their efforts on world balance and insisting that the disenfranchised get their fair share. The Millennial looks for direct solutions, and does not want to hear about answers that will take 100 years to come to fruition. They want to take action NOW. For those that decide to run for local, regional, or national office during their lifetimes, it is predicted they will focus on global issues, community balance, and on issues that relate to family and tradition.

Millennial Professionals are open-minded. More so than any other generation, Millennial Professionals are much more tolerant of different lifestyles (a majority of this generation supports gay marriage), different races, and different religions than previous generations. In terms of gay lifestyle acceptance, remember this is the first generation of kids to see "Gay Student Unions" at their high schools and witness same-sex couples attending the prom. Plus, they have grown-up seeing gay characters portrayed on television in a positive light, seen gay people on reality shows, and saw the launch of the first gay television network, LOGO. For a majority of Millennial Professionals, the gay lifestyle is just not an issue.

And, as I mentioned in the previous chapter, when it comes to racial diversity, recent polls have shown that over 80% of them are totally fine with marrying, or partnering with, someone outside their race. It also appears that an overwhelming majority support giving undocumented immigrants a chance to earn legal status and/or citizenship.

So, even though reports show that they are more conservative in terms of sex, vulgarity, and drugs than previous generations, they are more liberal in terms of tolerating and supporting alternative lifestyles, as well as different races and religions.

Furthermore, Millennial Professionals are highly aware of (global) political and environmental issues than previous generations (at their age). These kids and young adults freely express their opinions on political issues on their blogs, in chat rooms, and online forums, and not only with other people their age, but also with adults.

They are comfortable with their opinions, and are okay expressing them online for the world to see. This "comfort of expressing opinions" is something that we'll be discussing later, as it is critical to how you'll successfully work with them.

C H A P T E R   F I V E

The Relationship between Millennial Chicks & Millennial Guys

❖

This is the first generation of boys to be raised, in general, to respect girls as equals. And this is the first generation of girls raised to believe they ARE equals. These girls and young women, overall, do not "fear" speaking up around boys/men and they have been raised with boyfriends and boy *friends* that have always been (in general) respectful toward them and treated them equally.

If you're a GenX or Boomer, don't you remember that if you didn't have a date for the prom you didn't go? Well, the Millennials took that theory and chucked it out the window. Most kids now go to prom with a group of friends made-up of boys and girls. Boys and girls also hang out together as platonic friends, not just for romance. This is a very different dynamic than what GenX and Boomer kids experienced. The division of boys and girls was always apparent for those generations, and really, the only time the two "mixed" was based on dating.

Nowadays teenagers and young adults have best friends who are of the opposite sex and it's not "odd"; it's not uncommon to see a group of gender-mixed Millennials, all sitting on each other's laps, hanging on each other, hugging, etc. and none of them are dating, nor are they engaging in casual sex with each other. They are genuinely good friends that truly enjoy each other's company.

I have spoken to many Boomer and GenX parents with teenage children that said this whole concept was very odd to them at first, because it is completely different than what their childhood and adolescent experience was like.

This dynamic is important for employers to keep in mind. The new generation of employees entering the workforce is not typically "boy against girl." They are much more of the "we" mentality, and will be very comfortable partnering/collaborating with the opposite sex on projects.

Another perspective is that truly liberated women in society raised both genders of this generation. Their Boomer Moms and/or Grandmas were burning bras, marching for civil rights, and rallying for gender equality. Their GenX Moms entered the workforce in masses, and got men used to the fact that they will be in management and executive positions; not just secretarial roles. Their Boomer or GenX Moms saw Geraldine Ferrarro run as the Vice Presidential candidate with Walter Mondale on the Democratic ticket in the 1984 elections.

Approximately 75% of the 20-something Millennial Professionals had a working mother, and 25% come from a single parent household (typically a single mom). This generation of young adults has been raised by, and/or seen, strong women active-ly involved in career growth and in leadership positions their entire lives (at home and in the media!).

And, a majority of Millennial Chicks don't believe "they need a man" for happiness and security (as a large percentage of their grandmothers and mothers did when they were girls/young women). Millennial Chicks tend to believe that marrying a guy is a choice, not a necessity.

The relationships between the millennial genders, and their upbringing, are very important for employers to know. A group of young men is now entering the workforce that tends to have a lot of respect for women and is likely to shoot a sideways glance at a GenX or Boomer male counterpart that makes derogatory state-ments about female co-workers. Both genders are accustomed to female role models, so having a female boss isn't something that either sex will find as odd or problematic.

If anything, this new generation of young men is somewhat intimidated by their female Millennial counterparts, and they are used to these "chicks" speaking up and speaking out. Their relationship (in general) needs to be understood by your Boomer and GenX team members, because it may bring a new communi-cation and relationship dynamic into your work environment.

C H A P T E R   S I X

A Snapshot of Differences between Boomer, GenX, and Millennial Professionals

❖

In order for employers to understand the new dynamics their work environments are going to face, or are starting to face, it's important to understand the different players in the mix. Certainly, much of what you'll read are generalities, but this will give you a basic overview of how each generation in the workforce sees the world.

Also, keep in mind that there is always a two to five year range at the beginning and end of each generation's "time frame." As an example, on some timelines I'm considered one of the first GenXers, and on another I'm considered one of the last Boomers. But, as I mentioned before, one thing most experts agree on is the Millennial generation started in 1982, which is why their first graduating class of high school is considered the Class of 2000.

Quick Overview:

Boomers (approx. 1943 to 1960): Through my research, it seemed that most generational experts agree that Boomers tend to be optimistic and very driven. They are also viewed as having a love/hate relationship with authority and believe in leadership by consensus. Boomers also tend to identify closer with Millennial Professionals in terms of their "work together as a team" mentality.

GenX (approx. 1961 to 1981): GenXers tend to be the least like Millennial Professionals. And, since they will be working together longer in the workforce (as Boomers retire), getting them to understand each other will be critical to any work environment. Overall, GenXers are thought to be skeptical, desire a more balanced life, are unimpressed by authority, and are used to doing work tasks by themselves versus seeking a group effort. GenXers tend to be viewed as the "me" generation, where being self-centered and wanting "individual recognition" at work is a common trait. Millennial Professionals view the GenXers as curt, rude, and having a short fuse.

Millennial Professionals (1982 to 2002'ish): Millennial Professionals are perceived as hopeful, ambitious, and show signs of being comfortable with authority. They believe strong leaders need to be achievers and welcome (actually need) leadership (more on that later). One-trait employers will be happy to hear is that Millennial Professionals are perceived as *loyal*, which may make them easier to retain, compared to their GenX counterparts. However, and I'll repeat this again later: *They tend to be very loyal, but they expect loyalty in return, or they will be gone in a flash.*

Before we get into tips on recruiting, managing, and motivating them, here is something else employers need to keep in mind. In Chapter 14 of *Millennials Rising* (the book I mentioned before) the authors, Howe & Strauss, made the following prediction. What you should note is the fact that they made many other predictions back in 1991 about the Millennials that have practically ALL come true, so pay attention to this one in particular:

Millennials will fully possess the youth culture between 2002 and 2007. Sometime between 2007 and 2012, they will break out as a major national phenomenon...and whatever institutions the first Millennials newly occupy—from college to pop culture, from armed forces to union halls and voting booths—will receive the same media glare, parental obsession, and political intrusion that high schools felt in the late 1990s.

This prediction IS coming true. The period of 2007 to 2012 is NOW, and many of the "institutions" these young adults are choosing to occupy are companies like yours. And, based on the parental obsession mentioned, you had better treat them right, or their "hovering" parents may pay you a visit. I'm kidding, but you get my point. Millennial Professionals are a big deal, and they are your company's future.

CHAPTER SEVEN

Key Millennial Traits All Employers Need to Know

❖

I thought that providing a brief snapshot of common person-ality traits found among most Millennial Professionals would be helpful. Again, these are generalities, but are (12) traits that tend to be similar among them.

1. Millennial Professionals Are Nice: One thing that most employers will be happy to hear about the Millennial Professionals is that the word "nice" is something these young adults are. But, that doesn't mean "milk toast," "doormat," or "shy." As mentioned in Chapter One, they have been raised with rules from the begin-ning, and they are the first postwar generation that hasn't rebelled against society or their parents. However, they are strong-willed, opinionated, and expect to be treated with respect.

2. Millennial Professionals Are Multi-taskers: Most of them were raised with a busy schedule, and are the generation for whom the term "play date" was created. These young adults were raised playing sports, being involved in extra curricular activities at school, juggling active social calendars with friends, working part-time jobs, keeping up grades (because now you need higher than a 4.0 GPA...boy, did I graduate in time), and participating in volunteer programs. And, as they have reached adulthood, most of them continue to manage busy schedules and tend to be extremely good at organizing and multitasking.

3. Millennial Professionals Have Fast Minds: These young adults can process information on the Internet at lightning speed, and they believe that email is too slow and it's "something their parents do." They prefer to IM with their friends/colleagues and share/receive info and results quickly with others. They maintain and manage a large social circle via the Internet, cell phones, and PDAs (just as teenaged Boomers and GenXers did by talking for hours on the phone at night). Not only do they manage and maintain friendships where they live, but they also manage and maintain a social circle worldwide through community websites such as MySpace and FaceBook. This is a lot to process, and many Millennial Professionals do it with ease!

4. Millennial Professionals Are Optimistic, Even Though They Have Witnessed A Lot of Negativity: A vast majority of Millennial Professionals feel they will personally be successful and can improve the world. Their optimistic view is impressive, considering that older Millennial Professionals have witnessed horrific

tragedies in their lives (close to home and abroad) such as: The Oklahoma City bombing; the Columbine High School shooting; the Twin Towers falling in New York after the 9/11 attack; beheadings by terrorists online; the Iraq War; and most recently, the Virginia Tech massacre.

5. <u>Millennial Professionals Are Pack Animals:</u> Millennial Professionals like to be with people, and have been raised to work with others. It will be rare for an employer to find a Millennial Professional that is happy being alone. Most Millennial Professionals feel that working as a group is more productive, and joining forces to accomplish a goal is ideal. Although they tend to be very competitive, they also understand the importance of teamwork.

6. <u>Millennial Professionals Have A Strong Individual Spirit:</u> Like every generation before them, Millennial Professionals like to express themselves through fashion and style, and individuality is very important to them. The difference between them and previous generations is that they typically won't "conform" to your environment just to impress you (like previous generations did). So, employers must realize that the fashionable attire and hairstyles that may walk in the door for an interview (even in a corporate environment) may be a bit different than your "normal" business attire. This is a generation that includes many individuals who may have a nose piercing or spiky green hair, yet graduated from Yale with honors, and could be the brightest person of any age you've interviewed in years. They expect you to respect them as-is, and accept their individuality. This is truly a group of young adults that you can't be quick to judge by their external appearance.

7. <u>Millennial Professionals Like Balance:</u> Although they are willing to work hard, don't expect finding Millennial Professionals willing to work 60 hours per week (a lot) very easy. They feel that if you are always working 60+ hours per week, you're obviously not managing your time well. They feel it's too bad you take so long to get your work done. These young adults value the good life like their parents do, but are not willing to sacrifice time with family and friends to achieve it. They'll figure out how to achieve success on their own terms, not yours. We'll discuss this more in the "managing" chapter.

8. <u>Millennial Professionals Make Decisions on How Things Feel:</u> They grew up expressing their feelings and opinions. So, Millennial Professionals will typically ask themselves, "How does this make me feel?" If the answer is "Not good," you (as their employer) will hear about it.

9. <u>Millennial Professionals Are Goal Oriented:</u> It is not uncommon for Millennial Professionals to arrive to their first day on the job with a list of their goals pre-written. They have been on a schedule since they were born, with "goals" for each hour, day, and week carefully outlined by their parents and teachers. This is a generation that had DayTimers™ in grade school. They are accustomed to having structure that shows a clear path for an end result.

10. <u>Millennial Professionals Are Inclusive:</u> This goes back to their "pack animal" mentality. They expect to work in an environment that is inclusive of everyone and where everyone is treated fairly.

11. Millennial Professionals Are Confident: Remember, they were raised by a generation where "self-esteem" was paramount. GenX and Boomer parents read self-help books and instilled their findings on their kids. There were told they could be anything and achieve anything if they put their mind to it and worked hard. Millennial Professionals will be very irritated with you if you discount their ideas and opinions at work just because of their age.

12. Millennial Professionals Are Aware of Others: I mentioned this before, but it's worth repeating. Most Millennial Professionals were required to do volunteer work to graduate high school. This civic-minded nature has followed many of them into adulthood. As an employer, you are bound to see your Millennial Professionals asking to start a fundraising effort (or similar) that is backed by the company, and intended to help the community, or world, in some way. Embrace it and encourage all generations at your company to get involved!

See? They're not so bad! These personality traits should make you pretty happy...and relieved. But, Millennial Professionals do have some liabilities that employers are starting to see now that this new generation of young professionals joins their companies, so we'll discuss those in Part Three. Knowing their liabilities is important if you plan on successfully managing and motivating them!

PART TWO

Attracting, Recruiting & Retaining Millennial Professionals

❖

"To be successful today, recruiters will need a different skill set. Rather than be event planners who are transaction-oriented, they'll need to become more adept and comfortable with technology and the on-line world."

Greg Ruf, CEO of MBA Focus (.com), a consulting firm that promotes an online resume database to corporate recruiters seeking new M.B.A. grads

C H A P T E R   E I G H T

Innovative Ideas for *Attracting* Millennial Professionals

❖

As the quote opening this section said, you need to expand your mind outside of your old style of attracting talent and embrace technology. Sure, attending campus job fairs is still important and having in-person gatherings (like cocktail parties and lunches for candidates), but the Millennial Professionals have grown up with wires protruding from their bodies since day one. These young adults live in a virtual world AND a "human" world, so you need to communicate with them through both.

The purpose of this chapter is to give you a few examples of how to attract the best and the brightest Millennial Professionals in unique and innovative ways. I don't care if you use one idea, or all of them, but you'll need to add some sort of technology strategy into your overall recruitment mix. And, no, simply adding a career section to your current company website is NOT enough.

My suggestion? Schedule a meeting between the Marketing Department and HR/Recruitment Team at your company and brainstorm ideas. *Recruitment* needs to be driven by a marketing strategy, and technology needs to be one of the tools in your bag of tricks.

1. <u>Hand Out Company Information on Flash Drives:</u> Not much explanation required. It's unique and instead of paying for collateral printing, you can invest in handing out Flash Drives at recruitment events instead. And, not only can you load them with literature but you can load a promotional video about your company on them, too!

2. <u>Webinars for Q & A:</u> Setting up a webinar is easy and it allows candidates from all over the country (and world!) to learn about your company in an innovative way. It also enables candidates to talk to managers, and employees their own age, about the company, its culture, the region the company is located in, etc.

3. <u>Get on YouTube:</u> This is where many Millennial Professionals live! You need to have a presence on YouTube to generate awareness for your company. Authors@Google and Women@Google are good examples of how you can have a presence online in an interesting way. Google created these two talk shows and record them at Google. They have nothing to do specifically with recruiting, but they give Google a reason to be on YouTube and provide interesting content. Sure, Google has the sex appeal and is flooded with college grads wanting to work there, but you can get buzz for your company, too, if you come up with an innovative idea and broadcast it on YouTube.

Another way is to give your new Millennial recruits a video recorder and have them record themselves at work, their social world, and out in the region so people can get an idea of the activities available in the city where you are headquartered. Your new recruits can basically keep a video blog of their work and life experiences (set some boundaries) and they can build a following of other people their age online.

4. Podcast/Vidcast/Blog/Vlog: Same concept as above but you can host it on your company website, a podcast hosting environment (like Podomatic.com), MySpace and/or FaceBook. And depending on the tool, you can use video, audio-only, or written (blog).

5. Have a Company Presence on MySpace and/or FaceBook: See #4. These are other online communities where your target audience is. Have a company presence on both! Surf around these sites and you will see examples of how other companies are using them to attract the Millennial Professional demographic.

6. Text Message Campaigns: Invite candidates to events through text messaging campaigns. Gather their phone numbers through online contests or surveys and then build a database for text message communication. Use them to alert candidates about new job openings, big company news and much more. Again, have your Marketing Department team-up with your HR Department and get creative with online campaign ideas!

7. Check out CareerTV.com: A lot of well-known companies

have a presence on this site (GE, Disney, the FBI, and many more!). You can upload short promotional videos about your company and job candidates can view them. Candidates can also upload their video resumes there and your recruitment team can check out prospects.

8. <u>Company Videogame and/or Online Business/Task Simulation:</u> Some large companies are actually having videogames created using their brands to get in front of candidates in a creative way. Some of these games enable students to build companies, create/manage an investment portfolio, complete specific tasks, etc. Not only does this get their brand in front of (MBA and under grad) students in a creative but the companies can also assess the students with how they perform. So, behind the scenes, the companies are also using this strategy for finding good candidates early, and starting the recruitment dance early, with students they are impressed with.

9. <u>Video Resumes:</u> Millennial Professionals are comfortable on camera and are jumping on the video resume bandwagon like crazy. Mention that you accept video resumes in your recruitment materials and on your website. You can even promote a video resume contest and have prizes: Most creative, best produced, most original, etc. This can encourage more applicants, and get you some great media coverage and/or Internet buzz! One thing to note, however, you may want to check with your company's legal team to see if there could be any liabilities around this in terms of applicants being able to claim discrimination based on your ability to see their gender, race, etc. This is a new job application tool

so any (potential) "legal" issues around it have yet to unfold.

Those are some solid ideas for you to chew on. And other than a promotional video for your company, none of them are that expensive! They just require someone at your company to manage them, research them, and come up with content and concepts. Here's an idea…create a task force of Millennial Professionals <u>you have already hired</u> and delegate it to them! They'll probably figure out strategies faster than any of your Boomer or GenX employees and come up with some great ideas for utilizing the latest technologies available today for attracting their peers!

<u>BONUS Ideas:</u> The next three ideas are not "high tech", but they are innovative. They are simple strategies that you should also consider:

1. <u>Fun Social Events:</u> Companies are hosting creative events, like Lunch 2.0, to attract talent. This type of thing sprouted in Silicon Valley in an effort for a company to attract new engineers or other tech-related personnel. The purpose is to invite soon-to-be-grads from targeted colleges and invite them to a lunch where young engineers (employees) are available to answer questions, facility tours are provided, the CEO addresses them in a keynote, entertainment is provided, etc. Based on your company, you can determine how a concept like this may work for your recruitment efforts.

2. <u>Family Day:</u> Like it or not, their parents are playing a BIG role in their decision making process when it comes to job selection. It is NOT uncommon nowadays for recruiters to take

prospects AND their parents to dinners and lunches in an effort to snag the candidate. As I mentioned before, this generation is very close to their parents, and the "Helicopter Parents" who helped them select a college *are now helping them to select a job*. Recruiters are finding that impressing and schmoozing the parents is as important as schmoozing the candidate. It's true, so deal with it, embrace it and create strategies that support it. Aside from private dinners or lunch, *Family Days* are gaining popularity for parents to tour the facilities, meet employees, talk to managers and executives, etc.

3. <u>Home Office Allowance:</u> New grads are demanding workplace flexibility. Many have seen their parents working from home for almost a decade and they want this same type of flexibility. Plus, they are accustomed to being able to communicate whenever and wherever and have a hard time understanding why they need to be sitting in a cubicle everyday to do their job. So many companies are offering substantial allowances to new recruits enabling them to set-up a nice home office environment (furniture, equipment, etc.), and then they offer an on-going annual home office allowance so that the employee can purchase any new hardware, software and/or furniture that becomes available.

Having your employees working virtually may not work for your company's structure, but be prepared to consider it even on a part-time basis, or even one day per week.

CHAPTER   NINE

Hot Buttons for *Recruiting* Millennial Professionals

❖

To help you recruit this new generation of professionals, here is a snapshot of (16) hot buttons that you should consider adding to your recruitment materials, your recruitment discussions, and in actual job interviews with Millennial Professionals. Remember: They are interviewing you as much as you are interviewing them!

1. We Provide New Experiences & Exciting Opportunities: Millennial Professionals were raised in a fast-paced world and are used to processing a lot of information - fast. They want to know they won't get bored and you can provide a stimulating and exciting place for them.

2. Our Core Values Are "Integrity & Honesty": This generation has grown up very jaded by the media, bombarded by false adver-

tising claims and obnoxious infomercials, and seeing people in power get away with dishonest and/or downright illegal activities (e.g. politicians, celebrities, pro athletes, and corporate business leaders). Values such as *honesty and integrity* are high on their lists, and they don't want to work for companies (or people) that don't truly possess those values.

3. You'll Be Challenged Quickly: Remember the issue about "not paying their dues"? Well, this supports that. You'll need to think of ways to challenge them quickly, even if they are starting in your mailroom. If you don't have challenges for them quickly, then you'll need to be prepared to clearly outline how long it will take for them to reach the "next level" at your company where the real challenges will start.

4. We Provide a Very Structured Path for Advancement: Some GenX and Boomers were happy just to get the job, and they'd worry about advancement and future possibilities once they were on the job and learned the ins and outs of the company. The Millennial Professionals are a bit different. They want to know that you have a plan for them from Day One on the job, and what the path is to get where they want to go. Again, they grew-up with structure and knowing what the goal was for most every task.

5. We Offer a Flexible Work Environment: Millennial Professionals have (possibly) watched their professional parents work remotely and not have to report to an office every day. Granted, it may have taken their parents 30+ years to achieve this flexibility because technology has only recently allowed us to work

virtually, but they don't care about that. Plus, this is a generation that was (perhaps) attending some of their college courses virtually. To Millennial Professionals, the technology is HERE NOW, and they want flexibility in how and where they work. Many employers are going to have to trust that their new 20-something employees will get their work done, even if they are not sitting in their designated cubicles everyday from 9:00 to 5:00.

6. <u>We Reward Hard Work:</u> This goes back to praise. Be prepared to create "reward programs" or at least mention that your company truly values hard work and that their extra efforts won't go unnoticed. And then be sure to back that up with action. *This is a very important point that I'll discuss in more detail later.*

7. <u>We Provide a Fun Atmosphere:</u> I don't care if you are the most uptight financial institution in Boston, or the most sedate biotech company in San Jose, you had better start thinking about ways to have some fun. This doesn't mean having to paint your offices wild colors, buying pool tables, or allowing dogs in the office. But, the Millennial Professionals were raised being really active, having fun, and enjoying life. Your company needs to determine what can be done to add a little "festivity" to your culture, if it hasn't already, because Millennial Professionals, in all industries, won't do well in a stuffy environment.

8. <u>We Employ Fun & Friendly People:</u> This is similar to the point I made in #7, but they also want to know they will be surrounded by friendly co-workers. Millennial Professionals are

"pack animals" (remember?) and will be seeking new friendships and a social life within their new work environments. By the nature of who they are, their lines tend to get blurry between social life inside and outside of work.

9. <u>You Will be Treated With Respect & Your Opinions Valued:</u> Again, they don't want to feel disrespected just because they are new to the workforce and/or are the youngest people in your company. They need to be assured that your company will not treat them like entry-level "peons," and that your team is excited to hear their fresh, new perspectives.

10. <u>We Offer a Solid Mentoring Program & Strong Leadership:</u> I recently moderated a panel hosted by the Alliance for Technology & Women, and it was hosted by Yahoo. The topic was "Millennial Women in Technology" and the panel had 5 Millennial Chicks. I asked them what was one of the most important things they wanted in a work environment and ALL 5 of them answered *mentorship and guidance*. And, btw, these were bright young women with M.B.A.'s and all employed at big companies that you've heard of. So, if you don't have an official "mentoring program," emphasize that you (or their supervisor) will provide mentoring and are there to help them succeed at your company. Also mention that your managers and execs are strong leaders. Millennial Professionals were raised with a lot of handholding and guidance, and want to know your company offers solid leadership to help them achieve their goals. This is important to emphasize whether your company is a 6-person web design firm in Kansas or a Fortune 500 company in New York.

11. We Respect Your Personal Life: Millennial Professionals want to know that you don't expect their lives to become all about your company. They want assurance you will respect their lives outside of work and understand their need for a balanced life. Even in their 20's, they are highly aware of work-life balance.

12. We Support Entrepreneurial Spirit: This is a generation that embraces technology, is comfortable with constant change, and wants to be challenged. Let them know you welcome an entrepreneurial spirit, you welcome their ideas, and you expect them to think outside-the-box.

13. We Offer a Collaborative Work Culture: Millennial Professionals want to work with others and enjoy a team atmosphere. Emphasizing this will be important to them.

14. We Support & Encourage Advancement: Although this assurance is important to most any generation, it is very important to Millennial Professionals. They are seeing their whole lives before them and are excited about the future. Because they are goal-oriented, they want to know you support their desire to achieve great things and grow, personally and professionally.

15. We Support Diversity: Most Millennial Professionals grew up surrounded by different races, religions, cultures, and lifestyles. So, a majority of them will want to know your company supports, embraces and welcomes all types of people.

16. We Are Charitable & Green: As I mentioned before, they

are very pro-planet, pro-environment and pro-society (globally). Many of them want to work at a company that shares their same values and that wants to improve the world.

CHAPTER TEN

Unique Strategies for *Retaining* Millennial Professionals

❖

Congratulations! You have successfully recruited some great Millennial Professionals by using the ideas from chapters 8 and 9, right? But now the real work starts – you need to retain them! And, although they are loyal, they are only loyal if you treat them well. And how do you know if you're <u>not</u> treating them well? *They leave.*

This is not a generation that sits silently and suffers with the boss who is a jerk and that is just thankful to have a job. This is not a generation that feels rewarded by merely receiving a paycheck every 2 weeks and getting paid vacation time. Those were the things that made Boomers and GenXers feel "rewarded"...along with the occasional tacky award plaque presented at some cheesy annual company event or "Employee Recognition" potluck.

Sorry, Charlie, you can kiss those days good-bye! Millennial

Professionals want praise, feedback, and reward A LOT. And guess what? As you read this, companies are scrambling to think of innovative ways to turn into the ultimate "We Value YOU Culture". I strongly advise that you adopt this mentality company-wide, and enforce it at all levels of management, or you will be forced to replace your lobby's fancy glass door with a revolving one. This is going to seem really odd to many Boomer and GenX managers, but it is how this new generation is impacting the workforce. But the good news is it can be fun for everyone!

1. Again, become a "We Value YOU Culture": There are well-known companies assigning people to positions like "Thank You Coordinator" and "Rewards Manager". Companies have these people throwing confetti on people daily as recognition, handing out helium balloons to employees that have done a great job for something, giving special baseball hats to people that have done a task perfectly, etc. It goes on and on. I actually heard about one company that estimates that 1 out of its 400 employees receives praise every 20 seconds. They actually have the ability to measure their "praise rates"!

If you run short on ideas, I strongly recommend buying all your managers, and HR team, this book: *1001 Ways to Reward Employees*, by Bob Nelson, PH. D. I actually hand this book out as a gift when I conduct my HR Millennial Briefings and Managing Millennial Professionals Seminar for Boomer and GenX managers. It's loaded with great ideas and you can mix and match them so that your "praise" activities don't get old.

2. Team-Up Millennial With An Older "Partner": I don't liter-

ally mean one of the partners of your company, but another employee who is more seasoned than they are. So you can partner a new salesperson with an older one and they can team-up on accounts together. The older employee can show the newbie the ropes and the newbie can bring some fresh perspective into the sales process. After the newbie has been around a few years you can give that person a newbie to partner with.

3. Immediately Outline a 3/6/12 Month Plan: Millennial Professionals want a plan outlined for their career. I strongly advise managers to develop a plan within the first week of the Millennial Professional's employment and refer back to it with status meetings regularly. Simply telling them to work hard and they'll advance is not good enough.

4. Include Their Family & Friends: Many of your Millennial Professionals may not yet be married. I've heard that over 60% of recent college grads live at home, so encourage them to invite a friend or their parents to work events, like your annual company picnic or Holiday party. This is a small gesture that goes a long way in building loyalty and good will.

5. Support Work-Life Balance: I've mentioned this before but it's worth repeating. This generation is very aware of work-life balance and they expect a company to respect their lives outside of work. Combine this with your reward system! If you have a Millennial Professional employee that is into hiking, give him/her a gift certificate to an outdoor store and/or give them a 1/2 day off on a Friday to go hiking as a reward.

6. <u>Invent New (Fun) Company Policies:</u> I've heard about companies that enforced new policies like ending the workday at noon every Friday during the summer. So think about things like that and be open to new company policies that everyone, of all ages, will enjoy. These unique changes can attract AND retain Millennial Professionals.

7. <u>Assist With Life-Change Planning (and I don't mean menopause):</u> There are companies that actually have programs where they assist Millennial Professionals (who perhaps started with them at 22-23 years old and are now 26) make decisions about the next stage of their lives. Perhaps they are starting to think about marriage, children, buying their first home, etc. These are all big changes that many people in their mid-to-late 20's start to experience. It is a great idea to offer a guidance program around these life changes to help them with decision-making, and to explain how the company is there to help and support them.

Many Millennial Chicks I speak with start becoming concerned about their career and current job when they start thinking about having kids. It is a very stressful thing for career-oriented women. And if they feel that their current company won't support their choice to have kids, and/or they think that is will negatively affect their career with the company, they will begin seeking out a company whose culture <u>does</u> support working moms.

The "life changing programs" (for both male and female Millennials) can provide them with great info and support so that you can all go through their life changing experiences together and *keep your talent intact.*

8. Company Community Online Forum: Create an internal online community site where people can share ideas, seek help, brainstorm, troubleshoot ideas and concepts, create teams for projects, network internally for social activities, etc. Millennial Professionals are comfortable with this type of communication and will appreciate a virtual company community. Again, they are online communicators, they are pack animals, and they like to know that help/support is one click away.

9. Make Their First Day Memorable: I strongly recommend making the Manager of the new Millennial Professional, and/or the CEO (if you have a mid-size/smaller company), greet the newbie on his/her first day in the lobby. And I mean be there 10 minutes before the newbie is scheduled to arrive. Do not make the new Millennial Professional sign in at the front desk with a receptionist that doesn't know him/her, and then wait in the lobby for someone's *assistant* to come get them. Require that their boss is there to greet them, take them on a tour, introduce them to people, take them to lunch, have a special gathering of the department (or at least direct peer group) to meet/greet them on the first day, etc.

Just like their parents and society before you: Handhold them, coddle them, and make them feel special from Day One.

PART THREE

Managing & Motivating Millennial Professionals

❖

"This is the most high-maintenance workforce in the history of the world. The good news is they're also going to be the highest performing workforce in the history of the world."

Bruce Tulgan, founder of the leading generational-research firm RainmakerThinking, Inc. and author of *Managing Generation Y*

CHAPTER   ELEVEN

Common Complaints Employers Have About Millennial Professionals

❖

Although the Millennial Generation is said to be the brightest and best-educated generation our country has ever seen, and even though they typically far surpass their GenX and Boomer bosses and co-workers in the area of being tech-savvy, this unique group of young adults certainly isn't arriving into the professional world without their fair share of "baggage." Being told by the world you are "special" your entire life, being raised with a lot of structure, and being raised by doting parent(s), can come with a price.

This chapter is intended to give you a brief overview of the (8) most common complaints GenX and Boomer bosses have about this group of new employees. Again, these are generalizations, but they are common enough for me to mention.

I won't be providing suggestions about how to work with these liabilities until Chapter Twelve. There you'll get helpful management strategies to consider. But, in this brief chapter you'll get a basic overview that is bound to spark some management ideas of your own, based on who you are and your management style.

1. Millennial Professionals Require Structure & Supervision: This goes back to the point of them being raised with structured schedules, hovering parents, and hands-on teachers. Managers complain that although they are very independent and bright, they need to be given a clear path and plan for accomplishing a task. Regular "checking in" is needed by their supervisor to assist with obstacles, answer questions, and to provide guidance.

2. Millennial Professionals Are Impatient: They come from an upbringing where they didn't have to wait long for much of anything. "Instant gratification" became a popular buzz term in their lifetimes. Although they are willing to work hard, they tend to have a tough time with the concept of "paying your dues." If they are performing well at their jobs, they will expect quick recognition and rewards. And for many, the reward they seek is a promotion; they will not accept "age" as a reason for not getting promoted.

3. Millennial Professionals Have Trouble with Conflict: This circles back to being coddled and doted on by society, parents, teachers, relatives, and peers throughout their lives. They were raised to help, accept, and embrace their peers, and to talk about their feelings. This tends to be very different from GenXers and Boomers. GenXers and Boomers tend to be more edgy and abrupt, and have worked in business environments where yelling in a

meeting wasn't all that strange. But, raised voices, yelling, rude attitudes, condescending tones, and/or threats of being fired don't work well with this new generation. Those are management styles over which the Millennial Professionals will leave a job. This is different from how many GenX and Boomers were raised in the workforce. Those generations were taught not to challenge bosses, "keep your mouth shut regardless of how your boss speaks to you," and "just do your job."

4. Millennial Professionals Typically Don't Embrace Long Hours: Many employers may be shocked to find that finding tons of Millennial Professionals willing to work a 60 hour work week (regularly) will not be easy. As mentioned in previous chapters, these young adults are willing to work very hard while they are on-the-job, but are not willing to sacrifice time away from doing hobbies outside of work or spending time with friends and family. This is a different mentality than how most GenX and Boomers have been in the workforce. The Millennial Professionals want the "balance" that most GenXers are now striving for, but would not dare to ask for when they first started working. *The difference?* This new generation is asking for it upon entering the job market...not after working in it for 20+ years.

5. Millennial Professionals Seem to be Disrespectful of Superiors: Even though they tend to be polite, they are not stupid. If they have a manager that is clearly not very good at their job, and obviously not qualified, they will say something. Being older than them doesn't come with immediate respect, in their eyes. They need to see that their boss is truly a good leader, a respectful

manager, has something to teach them, and isn't hiding behind a "title." You expect them to prove themselves to you, and they expect the same from you.

6. Millennial Professionals Ask "Why?" A lot: Don't be surprised if you get "pushback" on your requests when managing them. Millennial Professionals want to know a reason for the request, the purpose, and the ultimate goal. Again, they are goal-oriented and have been raised with structure. Simply saying, "Because I said so" isn't going to be good enough with this new generation of employees. You can certainly choose to offer that reason, but you'll likely receive a resignation text message fairly quickly.

7. Millennial Professionals Are Outspoken: Yes, they are. They were raised to be confident and to share their feelings and ideas. They were also told that they are smart, bright, and special. Just because they will be new to your company doesn't mean they are suddenly going to become insecure or lose confidence in their ideas.

8. Millennial Professionals Need Constant Praise: This is very different for GenX and Boomer bosses. Doing a good job is *expected* in their world, and getting praise for every milestone isn't a typical management style for either of these generations. But, Millennial Professionals require constant feedback and don't want to wait for their annual review to get it. They have been raised with pats on the back daily from teachers and parents, so they will now expect it in their work environments, too. This plays a big part in keeping them happy and motivated, so buy a box of gold stars and

deal with it. And, don't get irritated with them about this…it was GenX or Boomer parents that raised them.

CHAPTER TWELVE

Solid Strategies for *Managing* Millennial Professionals

❖

Managing an individual, or group of similar individuals, that tend to be emotionally sensitive, in need of ongoing praise, that want guidance but also yearn for independence, who are accustomed to a hyper-stimulating lifestyle (fast communication technology, fast action in videogames, non-stop activity calendars, etc.), proves to be challenging for many of the GenX and Boomer bosses with whom I consult.

So, in this chapter, I'll outline (12) solid strategies that may help you manage the new generation of employees at your company. Many of these suggestions have helped other people prepare, handle, and deal with the Millennial monsoon that has hit their workplace.

1. Be Sensitive & Abandon a Curt Approach: An aggressive,

fairly typical GenX and Boomer management style will not fly with most Millennial Professionals. Managing by fear, threats, a raised voice, and egocentric style is going to have them either calling you on it or leaving. Many GenX and Boomer professionals kept their mouths shut with bosses that managed like that, but not Millennials. So, if you have been told you are rough around the edges, this might be a good time to adjust your approach and get a grip.

2. Treat Them with Respect: This advice can go hand-in-hand with #1, but it even transcends managing them. Millennial Professionals want to be treated with respect, even if they are young and/or inexperienced. Share this with your other employees that are not their managers. Basically, it's time for your entire company to become a bit more sensitive and respectful of others (if it isn't already).

3. Get to Know Them Personally (outside interests, hobbies, etc.): With Millennial Professionals, more than with any other workforce generation, it is important to take the time to get to know them individually. Personally, I have always been like this as a manager, regardless of the employee's age, and it has served me well. I've been fortunate enough to suffer from very little turnover and have key employees that have been with me 10+ years. With Millennial Professionals you can use this knowledge to help them make personal plans for achieving balance between work and home. For instance, if your Millennial Professional really enjoys yoga, and you know his/her favorite yoga class starts at 5:00 two nights per week, let her/him leave early on those days to catch the

class. Small gestures like that go a LONG way in building loyalty and respect.

4. Encourage Them to Share Ideas & Speak-up at Meetings: Although we have talked a lot about Millennial Professionals being confident, that may become a bit different in a new work environment where, for the first time in their lives, they are not surrounded by friends, teachers, or parents. So, it would be good to help your new younger employees understand how meetings at your company work (before having them attend one) by explaining what to expect, and by providing a meeting outline prior to each meeting so they can have some time to prepare and participate. Again, they are typically "planners." Providing them with meeting agendas prior to the day of the meeting would work well with their personalities.

5. Set-up Your Work Environment for Idea Sharing: If your office space is all cubicles and private offices, you would be served well by adding an area of small tables and chairs, or couches, where people can casually gather to discuss projects. If you employ quite a few Millennial Professionals, you may even want to consider removing cubicle walls and opening up your space for more collaborative engagement. Remember, they are pack animals and enjoy working in groups. Provide an environment that encourages that.

6. Coach About Establishing Credibility in the Company: This advice is important if you are in a medium to large company. Coach your new Millennial Professional(s) about what builds credibility

in your company and what other managers and executives expect from employees. The brighter your employee(s) shine, the better you look as their manager. Coach them on navigating the waters of your company, and help them become respected contributors to the department and/or company overall.

7. Establish Training, Mentoring and Even Reverse Mentoring Programs: This is important so I'm repeating it in this chapter because it's a good for recruiting them, motivating them, AND retaining them. Millennial Professionals want strong leadership and seek environments that teach them new things on a regular basis. They want stimulation, and have been raised with an abundance of it; more than any other generation!

They will get bored quickly, so if you can't create new things for them to learn often, be willing to send them to seminars and workshops, off-site as well as online. Find topics that will enhance their career in your industry as well as make them more valuable to you. Is there new project management software you've wanted to implement at your company for a long time, but have been too busy to get it set-up? Delegate that task to a Millennial Professional and have them run with it!

Aside from appointing your new employees to a mentor to help *them* learn the ropes and have a person to go to with questions/issues, I read about a great idea called a "Reverse Mentor" program. For example, you can assign a Millennial Professional to an older employee that is less tech-savvy, and have the Millennial mentor *them*. This is win/win for everyone: Your Millennial Professional feels respected and needed, and your GenX or Boomer team members can overcome their (possible) fear of the latest technology advances and can become more productive for your company.

One last example is to arrange for your Millennial Professional to "shadow" different managers and/or execs in various departments within your company. Each month have them shadow someone in a different department for one to three days. This doesn't cost your company anything, and can spark ideas in your Millennial Professionals about ways the company can integrate processes, partner on projects, etc. It keeps them stimulated and engaged, without being too disruptive to business.

8. Be Open-minded: Some of the best ideas for setting up a new process has been from Millennial Professionals. They arrive with fresh perspective, fast minds, and (typically) an organized way of thinking. Rather than be irritated with a suggestion to change a process your company may have implemented for years, be open to hearing new ideas. Basically, be open to hearing ideas on just about anything, because I have found that a majority of the time it adds value.

9. Be Clear & Concise, But Allow Freedom to Determine Best Route: Explain to them what you want accomplished, and then get out of the way. Check-in often, but don't micro manage. Ask for up-dates based on the timeframe to which you both agreed.

10. Challenge A lot & Delegate: This is really critical to managing and motivating a Millennial Professional. They were not raised to "get lost in cubicle land" and just collect a paycheck every two weeks. They want to make a difference, they want to be

challenged, and they want responsibility. When one task/project is done, have more lined-up and ready to go, and make them harder. A Millennial Professional will tell you when it's too much or when they need help. Until then, keep them challenged, non-stop.

11. <u>Be a Good Leader & a Team Player:</u> They have been raised with positive role models and expect them at work. If you think your leadership skills need some work, then this is the time to hone your skills. This generation craves strong leadership, and will not respect you, or stay with your company, if you don't provide it. If you have spent most of your time managing from your private office, rarely engaging with your team, time to come down from your ivory tower. Millennial Professionals tend to be team players and want a boss that demonstrates the same value. Popping in and out of your office to bark an order or firing off emails to delegate a task is not something to which they are accustomed. They want managers who don't appear to be "mightier than thou," and that truly provide *healthy* leadership, versus hide behind a smoke screen of ineptitude or throw egocentric attitude. Although GenX and Boomer employees also (normally) feel this way about their bosses, too, Millennial Professionals usually won't tolerate it as the generations before them do/have.

12. <u>Have Fun & Show Your Sense of Humor:</u> Putting on your hard-to-read, keep-a-distance management face may need to be reevaluated with this new generation. Many Millennial Professionals grew up calling teachers by their first names, having a say in their families' affairs, and being treated with a certain level of equality by adults. They prefer bosses that can show their true

colors (and I don't mean coming to work and airing your personal issues). So, if you're fun with your friends and family, then be willing to show that side of yourself more at work. Being a good leader doesn't mean you have to only show yourself in a serious light. In the eyes of a Millennial Professional, your credibility and respect level will skyrocket if you not only manage them with friendliness, but with a sense of humor (and *humanness*), as well.

CHAPTER THIRTEEN

Sound Solutions for *Motivating* Millennial Professionals...and a Handful of Guaranteed Motivation Busters!

❖

Many companies I speak with have trouble in the area of motivating their Millennial Professionals. The standard motivator of "work hard and you'll get a raise or promotion" that has worked for decades on GenX and Boomer employees is simply not enough to motivate this new generation of employees. The older generations' attitudes of just being thankful to have a job and/or working hard just for status also aren't huge motivators for them. Millennial Professionals want to feel like they are contributing for a reason, and they want to see there are clear goals and rewards for what they are asked to do. Money isn't always the biggest motivator.

So, I have put together (8) sound solutions that companies I have consulted with have found to be very helpful. Millennial Professionals are seeking more than a regular paycheck, two weeks vacation, benefits, and an occasional raise or promotion...so keep reading!

1. <u>Find out What Motivates Them:</u> Sounds simple, but many managers don't do this. If your Millennial Professional is an avid snowboarder, offer up a new snowboard or lift tickets as rewards for a goal. Even though it is "about money" it takes on a new excitement if it's customized for their personal interests versus a cash bonus. I occasionally give female employees gift certificates for manicures and pedicures just as a "thank you" gesture for their hard work and you'd think I'd given them winning lottery tickets with how thrilled they get.

2. <u>Map Their Personal Goals Back to Tasks:</u> Find out what they want out of their jobs and what gets them excited. Try to map those back to tasks/projects you give them. This enables you to explain how this task relates to their job advancement and allows you to "sell them" on the importance of doing it. Upon completion, you can go over what they accomplished and discuss how it benefits them.

3. <u>Clearly Outline Goals & Rewards for Everything:</u> Be very clear on what you want done and what they will get when it's done. For instance, if you ask your entry-level Millennial Professional (that aspires to be a salesperson at your company) to create a prospect database for a new industry you want to pursue, tell them you expect it to have 500 companies in it, and they have 30 days to complete the task. Upon completion, their reward will be to shadow your top salesperson for five days, with the possibility of

the Millennial Professional personally contacting 25 of the prospects from the database he/she created. Even if you know this person won't be ready for sales for a year or more, you've accomplished two things with this reward: One, it gives him/her a chance to see early on if a sales position is something that really interests them, and two, you have given them a reward that offered "more responsibility," even if it was only to contact 25 prospects.

As you can see, rewards don't always have to be about "fun" gifts or cash bonuses. I actually think that a majority of rewards throughout the year should be things that relate to, or benefit, your company (like shadowing the top salesperson).

4. Recognition: Millennial Professionals were raised getting certificates and kudos all through school. Even if their little league team came in last, they still got a trophy. Again, I suggest purchasing this book for ideas: *1001 Ways to Reward Employees*.

5. Create a Fun Culture: Take a poll and ask if your employees think you have a fun and/or enjoyable work environment. If the answer is not positive, ask a Millennial Professional to head-up a "task force" to brainstorm what could make things more enjoyable. If you have a workforce with a diverse group of ages, require that two to three people from each generation be asked to join.

6. Encourage Them to Recruit Their Friends: You need to deal with the fact that, as the years go by, your work environment is going to become a more "friend" oriented place. As I mentioned in previous chapters, Millennial Professionals have close friendships and enjoy being with their friends *a lot*. They will want to create

these types of relationship in the workplace, too, so capitalize on this by encouraging them to recruit their friends. Even consider creating a "Refer a Friend" recruitment program.

7. Don't Delay Feedback: This is the "instant gratification" generation that expects to hear positive praise right away. If a Millennial Professional has done a good job, tell them immediately and also share *why* it was such a good job. Also, use words with a bit more excitement versus the standard "Good job!" Something like "What you did is really *awesome!*" is more along the lines of the colorful praise with which they are familiar.

8. Make a Reward *Increased Responsibility*: I know I'm beating a dead horse here, but you need to understand this. Millennial Professionals grew-up on a steady diet of fast moving videogames, hectic schedules, text messaging at the speed of light, and a bazillion cable stations to surf. Many have the attention span of a gnat on a triple shot of espresso, so you have to be creative with ways to challenge and engage them. New challenges and constant stimulation keeps them motivated. This doesn't mean constantly having to promote them! Find ways to challenge them within their current positions until they *deserve* to be promoted.

A Handful of Guaranteed Motivation Busters: Here are a few ways to quickly squelch their motivation and have your Millennial Professionals heading for the nearest exit: Don't give them advancement opportunities; don't provide on-going training and learning opportunities; do enforce strict rules and rigid schedules; do judge them based on appearance; do try to strip them of their individuality and make them conform into a Stepford employee; be inflexible with flex-time and/or the ability to work remotely (even if you allow it on occasion is good, but I know this depends on your company's overall work environment); and rarely praise or reward them for doing an *awesome* job.

PART FOUR

A Global Perspective
PLUS Two Bonus Chapters

"Special thanks to Yahoo! HotJobs and Robert Half International for their contribution to this section. And also a big shout out to the members of the Employee Engagement Network for their contributions. I'd also like to thank myself for writing the chapter about Millennials around the world. Without me, I couldn't have done it."

Lisa Orrell, Millennial & Generations Relations Expert, author of *Millennials Incorporated*, speaker, author, consultant, Mom, and just a great person who is a legend in her own mind

C H A P T E R   F O U R T E E N

A Global Perspective: Are Millennials the Same Around the World?

❖

I am asked this a lot. And here's my brilliant short answer: "Yes, they appear to be the same in many areas of the globe." So, regardless of where you are located on Planet Earth, you can still benefit from the first three sections of this book! I suppose that I could just end this chapter here but I'll give you a bit more info.

Although there are exceptions to every rule, recent research shows that the Millennial personality traits and workforce demands that we are seeing in the U.S. are permeating into other cultures. My belief is that over time we may not even be referring to this generation as the "Millennials", but rather the "Global Generation". And with the popularity of social networks, and the ability to communicate with people all around the world, it's not a surprise that the Millennial's workplace expectations are similar around the globe. Plus, we have many students going to other countries for their college education and they inherit ideals from each other.

That last factoid brings up a good point (on a total side note): One of the other things that will be affecting the U.S. labor shortage, that I mentioned in the Introduction of this book, is that we are seeing a trend where students from countries (like China and India) come to the U.S. for college BUT more and more of them are choosing to go back home when they graduate. The era of "the United States is THE best and only place to live" is waning. Many young adults see positive changes and opportunities in their homelands, and are returning there after graduating from a U.S.-based college to start their careers, start businesses, and start their families.

Okay, back to the question about them being the same. Another interesting aspect to this is that regardless of what type of upbringing and experiences the <u>parents</u> of Millennials around the globe experienced growing up, the Millennials in a wide variety of countries are similar. So this "global generation" seems to be being shaped more *by the influence of each other around the world* versus by the total influence of their homeland cultures and parents' beliefs and life experiences. Simply put, it's as if the Boomer's child rearing of the Millennials in the U.S. has now also influenced Millennials in other countries.

Millennial Professionals around the planet seem to want: Strong managers, mentor programs, praise, rapid career paths, flexible work environments, fun in the workplace, to be challenged in their jobs quickly, work/life balance, good pay, AND to *feel valued*. And when Millennials are not receiving these things from employers in the U.S., or elsewhere, they look for a new job.

So, it's true, many of the challenges U.S. companies face with recruiting, managing and retaining Millennials are also challenging MANY other companies based in other countries. To that point, I'm in the early stages of collaborating with Mark McCrindle in Australia, a trained Psychologist and Social Researcher. He is also a Millennial expert who conducts seminars similar to mine for companies in countries such as: Australia, Japan, Singapore, Malaysia, China, and Thailand. And why are they hiring him? Because they are facing the same challenges as U.S. companies! That's one snippet of proof that I'm not making this stuff up.

What other countries refer to them as Millennials? This is another question that I get a lot. I recently conducted my *Global Millennials Seminar* for a group of executives from the Global Diversity Team of a large technology company in the U.S. (with offices worldwide). In gathering research for the seminar, here is the answer to that popular question (broad answer): Canada, APAC (China, Australia, New Zealand and India), and EMEA (most of Europe and Africa). The media in Fiji has also used Generation Z, and the media in Pakistan has also referred to them as the Global Generation.

I have read many articles on this topic filled with quotes from executives in other countries that are *identical* to the observations you read/hear from executives in the U.S. regarding their Millennial employees. I actually present some of those quotes in my seminars, without telling where the person is from, and make the audience guess the country. Any one of the quotes I show could be from a U.S. manager. But they're not. The quotes I share are from senior executives and front line managers in companies based in Nigeria, Hong Kong, Argentina, India, Mumbai, South Africa, and Kenya (to name a few).

Our world has never seen an entire generation of young people who are so similar around the globe. We really are turning into a world without borders, with a global workforce of 20-somethings that can relate to each other…and that now expect the same things from their employers.

BONUS
CHAPTER FIFTEEN

Success Defined: What Gen Y Wants in a Career

Special thanks to Yahoo! HotJobs and Robert Half International for providing this bonus chapter from their Special Report: *What Millennial Workers Want: How to Attract and Retain Gen Y Employees.*

"Generation Y Professionals favor a laid-back but very efficient manager who will help them with their professional growth"

Trina White, 26, Marketing Assistant

CHAPTER FIFTEEN

Success Defined: What Gen Y Wants in a Career

❖

I was thrilled when Yahoo! HotJobs and Robert Half International granted me permission to reprint a section from their Special Report, *What Millennial Workers Want: How to Attract and Retain Gen Y Employees*, as a bonus chapter for my book.

Keep in mind this is only <u>one section</u> from their extensive report, and you can download the entire document (for FREE!) by going to: www.rhi.com/GenY.

Based on "rules" stated by their legal teams, the following content is in its original state, so the first sentence may not make sense...there is a section that comes before this information in the complete Special Report.

Success Defined: What Gen Y Wants in a Career

Now that we know what Generation Y looks for in a job offer, let's consider what they want in their careers over the long term – keeping in mind that "long" for these professionals means years, not decades. More than half of those surveyed believe they should spend just one to two years "paying their dues" in entry-level positions. Moreover, nearly half (43 percent) of Gen Y workers surveyed said they plan to stay between one and five years at their current jobs, while only 22 percent expect to spend six or more years in the same position.

To retain your Gen Y workers, focus on the work environment. Workplace factors that are most important to Gen Y are working with a manager they respect and people they enjoy, and striking a balance between personal and work obligations.

"How much time do you think professionals entering the workforce should have to spend 'paying their dues' in entry-level positions?"	
Less than one year	16%
One to two years	51%
Two to three years	19%
More than three years	5%
Not sure	9%

"How long do you expect to stay at your current position?"	
Less than one year	16%
One to two years	24%
Three to five years	19%
Six years or more	22%
Not sure	19%

Gen Y respondents ranked the following aspects of their work environment on a one-to-10 scale, with 10 being the most important, and one least important:	
Working with a manager I can respect and learn from	8.74
Working with people I enjoy	8.69
Having work/life balance	8.63
Having a short commute	7.55
Working for a socially responsible company	7.42
Having a nice office space	7.14
Working with state-of-the-art technology	6.89

The Boss Factor

As with professionals of all ages, the quality of a Gen Y employee's relationship with his or her manager is directly linked to job satisfaction. Remember that Millennials are accustomed to direct, ongoing supervision and guidance from parents, teachers and other authority figures. They seek a similar relationship with their bosses, looking to them for almost constant feedback. In fact, 35 percent of those surveyed want to communicate with the boss several times a day. Once per day is sufficient for one-quarter of respondents, while only 10 percent would be content with weekly communication.

Portrait of a Gen Y Dream Boss
- A skillful manager, advisor and supporter
- Pleasant and easy to get along with
- Understanding and caring
- Flexible and open-minded

Clearly, this generation, like most workers starting their careers, has high ideals when describing the types of supervisors they seek. Trina White, a 26-year-old marketing assistant, sums it up this way: "They want a laid-back but very efficient manager who will help them with their professional growth.

"For me, the ideal manager has clear expectations and takes time to meet with me so that we can update each other about what we are working on and what needs to be done," White says. "He or she needs to be able to give suggestions without being too critical, be able to help me grow and guide me in my professional development, and be a mentor. A good manager also needs to be respectful of my time and trust me to get the job done."

By contrast, Generation Y's "nightmare boss" is, according to White, "a micromanager who is not concerned with my professional development, and who tends to place blame on everyone other than him/herself."

In essence, being a good manager to Generation Y means being a good manager – period. After all, who wouldn't want to work for a supportive coach and mentor? But for Millennials, having a good boss is particularly important. This is a group that has high expectations for authority figures and craves continual feedback and reinforcement. Pairing these staff members with your best managers will go a long way toward keeping these employees satisfied and productive.

Gen Y respondents were asked, "How would you describe your dream boss?"

- Good management skills
- Pleasant and easy to get along with
- Understanding and caring
- Flexible and open-minded
- Respects/values/appreciates employees
- Good communication skills

Following are some additional management tactics that may help you bring out the best performance in your Gen Y staff:

Give them their "scores."

Recent graduates are accustomed to receiving regular feedback in the form of test scores and grades and appreciate knowing where they stand. Don't wait for the annual performance review to provide feedback – give "spot reviews" as tasks and projects are completed. Immediate input on their performance and progress will help motivate these team members.

Keep the door open, but don't be a doormat.

This group appreciates a friendly, fair-minded manager who dispenses advice, provides support and then gives them space to do their jobs in their own way. But they aren't looking for pushovers: They want their supervisors to exercise clear authority.

Give it to them straight.

This was not a "children-should-be-seen-and-not-heard" generation. As youngsters, they likely questioned things and received fairly open responses. Subsequently, Millennials expect honesty and candor from their managers.

Walk the talk.

Similarly, this group wants companies to act true to their values. They are skeptical of corporate pronouncements unless they are backed up with clear action.

See them as people, not just employees.

Like all professionals, these workers want supportive managers. When talking with Gen Y staff members, acknowledge that they have lives and concerns outside of work, and help them balance work and personal obligations.

> **73%: Nearly 3-out-of-4 Gen Y workers polled are worried about balancing work and personal obligations.**

Lend them your ears.

They seek the validation that comes from being heard. This does not mean that you have to act upon their every suggestion, but you can acknowledge their ideas and encourage them to approach you with their thoughts.

The Coworker Factor

While Internet technology has been fairly ubiquitous for this group, don't assume it's their communication method of choice. This is a highly sociable generation, accustomed to doing things as part of a group since their years in daycare and preschool. Perhaps that's why two-thirds of survey respondents selected in-person conversations with their coworkers as their preferred communication method. Only one in five would rather communicate by e-mail.

The takeaway for businesses: Make sure your workplace is structured to encourage plenty of the kind of "face time" that Gen Y professionals enjoy. This could mean arranging work groups in open, connected seating areas that facilitate face-to-face communication or creating more opportunities for employees to socialize during and after work. Pleasant break rooms or cafeterias, monthly staff lunches and opportunities to socialize away from the office can go a long way toward keeping this group engaged and productive. If Gen Y professionals feel connected to their co-workers, they're more likely to be satisfied with their jobs and stay with your company.

"Let's Meet at the Water Cooler"

Surprise! Two-thirds of the "wired generation" favor in-person conversations with coworkers over other types of communication.

The Power of Balance

Nearly three-quarters (73 percent) of Gen Y professionals are concerned about being able to balance a career with personal obligations. You'll encourage longer tenures and greater loyalty among employees if you offer perks and programs that help them achieve work/life balance. This may require you to rethink traditional career paths or timetables for advancement, or offer options such as job-sharing, telecommuting, compressed work-weeks or alternative scheduling, when appropriate.

When Evaluating Employers, Gen Y Professionals Look For:
- **A manager they can respect and learn from**
- **People they can enjoy working with**
- **Work/life balance**

No Corner Offices

In keeping with their preference for an informal and friendly workplace, members of Generation Y are not particularly impressed by prestigious titles and fancy offices.

Dressed to Work...How Gen Y Wants to Dress on the Job:
- **Business Casual: 41%**
- **Sneakers and jeans: 27%**
- **A mix, depending on the situation: 26%**
- **Business attire: 4%**

Consider these survey results: Job title ranked seventh among 11 factors that Gen Y uses to evaluate a job opportunity. And they ranked a "more prestigious job title" last among seven factors that would prompt them to leave their current jobs. Generation Y employees are far more interested in challenging duties. In other words, it's what they do, not what they're called, that counts. Perhaps that's not surprising from a group that was commonly asked, "What do you want to do when you grow up?" versus "What do you want to be?" – a more common query for generations before them.

Gen Y respondents ranked how much the following factors would influence them to leave one job for another on a one-to-five scale, with five having the most influence, and one the least:	
Higher pay	4.63
Better perks and benefits	4.44
More opportunities for advancement	4.22
More interesting work	4.14
Better work environment	3.99
Shorter commute	3.51
More prestigious job title	3.39

Survey Methodology: For the entire Special Report (not just this section)

The survey was conducted in the second quarter of 2007 by an independent research firm. It includes a total of 1,007 web interviews of people 21 to 28 years old who are employed full-time or part-time and have college degrees or are currently attending college. Among those surveyed, 505 were males, and 502 were females. The majority of respondents (79 percent) were college graduates employed full-time; the rest were employed part-time and/or still attending college.

DOWNLOAD THIS ENTIRE SPECIAL REPORT FOR FREE!
www.rhi.com/GenY

BONUS
CHAPTER SIXTEEN

The Key ABC's of Employee Engagement

❖

Special thanks to the 12 contributing co-authors/experts
from the *Employee Engagement Network* for their shared
content in this bonus chapter:

David Zinger, Tim Wright, Terrence Seamon, Steve Roesler,
Lisa ForsythRaven Young, Robert Morris, Ken Milloy, Stephen
McPherson,George Reavis, Ian Buckingham and Angela Maiers

www.employeeengagement.ning.com

B O N U S
C H A P T E R   S I X T E E N

The Key ABC's of Employee Engagement

❖

Employee engagement is critical for successfully managing and motivating employees from ANY generation. So luckily I came across a terrific e-book where 12 experts contributed their personal ABC's for successful employee engagement, and I felt their tips would resonate well with your Millennial employees.

They were kind enough to grant me permission to share their (partial) content from the original e-book in this bonus chapter.

The original e-book has A-Z lists from EACH author and is filled with <u>over 300 tips</u>! But including all that content in this chapter would have added too many pages, so I chose to create the alphabet by using only a few tips from each author.

You now have the *condensed* employee engagement alphabet from A to Z, but you can download (for FREE!) the entire e-book online. Hey, 300 tips for free? Why not download it? Here's where you can find the e-book: www.davidzinger.com/ABC.pdf

But before you dive in to this chapter, here are some ideas about how you can use this alphabet (these ideas are particularly useful when reading their complete e-book):

Possible Applications

- Scan the authors to get ideas

- Use it as you begin to create your own alphabet

- Use it to launch a team or project group exercise on engagement

- Pick a letter each day and focus on that letter to enhance your own engagement or the engagement of others.

- Share it with others at work

- Offer it as a free resource during employee engagement sessions

- Develop your own applications based on your interest and focus on employee engagement.

❖

ABC's of Employee Engagement

A-B
by David Zinger:

Acceptance: We must begin with acceptance of the current state of engagement and begin to make changes out of our full acceptance of what is as we move to what can be.

Benefits: If employee engagement is to be sustained over time it must benefit employees, leaders, managers, organizations, and customers.

C-D
by Tim Wright

Circumnavigate: A straight line is the shortest distance between two points, but it's not always fastest or easiest. Prepare to go around obstacles. As you plan your engagement strategy, include contingencies that will get you past hindering situation, policy, and/or individual.

Document: Keep a journal of your employee engagement efforts and successes. You may hand your job over to someone at some point. You may derive new ideas from past successes. You may have to explain or defend engagement actions you've taken with your people. You may just enjoy reading about you've done.

E-F
by Terrence Seamon

Energize: Get excited and others will catch it!

Fun: If you aren't having fun, figure it out!

G-H
by Steve Roesler

Glad: We take time to celebrate when good things happen.

Harpoon: When something starts to drag us down, we nip it in the bud.

I-J

by Lisa Forsyth

Instruction: Teach the core beliefs and values of engagement to everyone in the organization.

Judgment: Judgment plays a critical role in effective leadership, and poor judgment can undermine any leader's success. Be judicious. Understand what is critical to your people and organization, take all known facts and perceptions into account, and communicate the meaning behind decisions made. Make judgments visible. Engage your people in decision-making. Teach them the basis of making sound judgments by involving them in the process where such judgments are made. Share an error in judgment with your team and encourage feedback that reveals errors in judgments, for these too are development opportunities for everyone.

K-L

by Raven Young

Keys: "All one has to do is hit the right *keys* at the right time and the instrument plays itself." — *Johann Sebastian Bach*

Learn: "The more that you read, the more things you will know. The more that you *learn*, the more places you'll go." — *Dr. Seuss*

M-N
by Ken Milloy

Meaning: My work has to have meaning. I am here for much more than a paycheck and to spend my day with others. I want to contribute and in return I want to gain. Work with me on building that meaning, on linking it together with our goals, and you will really begin to capture me, my heart, and my mind.

Notice: Take notice of what I do and how I do it. Better yet - take notice of *what all of us do* (individually and collectively), and give us credit for our efforts and achievements. Taking notice goes a long way. Oh...don't forget that taking notice means that you actually share with me that you noticed.

O-P
by Robert Morris

Objective: Prior to making a decision or reaching a conclusion, it is imperative to obtain as much information as possible from as many different sources as possible, and rigorously evaluate the information. "Prejudice" means pre-judgment. Challenge all assumptions and premises. Be open-minded. *Then take appropriate action.* The doing-knowing gap" probably causes as much damage as the "knowing-doing gap."

Potential: Darrell Royal once said that "potential" means, "You ain't done it yet." Merely advocating engagement does not achieve it.

Q-R

by Angela Maiers (perspective from an educator whose tips apply to the business world as well...we're all students!)

Questions: Questions that stretch student minds, invite curiosity, provoke thinking, and instill a sense of wonder, keep students engaged. Successful student engagement requires a classroom culture that invites mutual inquiry, gives permission to investigate open-ended and suggestive questions

Relationships: To grow 'em you must know 'em! Knowing our students seems obvious, yet many students claim that we do not "get" them. Students want and need a relationship with us. They work harder and smarter when they know that *their* learning matters to *us*. When students feel valued, honored, and respected, there is an interest and energy in the process of learning that reaches far beyond the content we teach.

S-T

by George Reavis

Share: This is the fifth of the 5 steps in the process, or recipe, in building employee engagement. Sharing helps build and maintain the *people connections* that create enjoyment for everyone involved. The other critical result of sharing is to facilitate assessments. Assessments are nothing more than opinions but, unlike measurements, they foster a dialogue or two-way discussions among all parties.

Thank: This is key to recognition, appreciation, and gratitude. Beneficiaries of your group's efforts will not remain engaged and reengage your group members if they are not thanked both verbally and non-verbally. "Thanking" is a pivotal step or action for any group leader to lead the engagement of their members.

U-W
by Stephen McPherson

Unanimous: Unanimously engage your physical, emotional and spiritual self.

Valor: Valor is the action of the truly engaged.

Winning: Winning is only possible through complete engagement.

X-Z
by Ian Buckingham

X: The generation who are responsible for much of the engagement activity.

Y: The generation who are responsible for translating much of the engagement activity.

Z: *Zoo!* Whatever formal engagement strategies there may be it's always going to be a fantastic, colorful jungle out there with grapevines aplenty, so open those cages and connect with the people!

❖

Get your FREE copy of the complete e-book, *The Keys of Employee Engagement*, <u>with over 300 useful tips,</u> by going here: www.davidzinger.com/ABC.pdf

Contact Info for Each Contributing Expert (great resources for you!):

David Zinger
President of Zinger & Associates
Employee Engagement Consultant, Coach & Speaker
www.DavidZinger.com

George Reavis
Founder of ThankingCustomers.com
Employee Engagement Practitioner
www.ThankingCustomers.com

Stephen A. McPherson
Consultant @ Peak Performance Systems
Leadership, management instructor & coach for top results
www.ppsgta.com

Tim Wright, CEO of Wright Results, Inc.
Employee Engagement Expert
www.CulturetoEngage.com
www.WrightResults.com

Lisa Forsyth
Director, Tactical Development, MSNBC.com
Student of Leadership & Engagement
www.LisaForsyth.com

Terrence Seamon
Portfolio Manager: American Management Association
Learning & OD Expert
http://learningvoyager.blogspot.com

Raven Young
Senior Project Manager
Project Management & Soft Skills Development Blogger
www.RavensBrain.com

Ken Milloy

President & Senior Consultant, Strategic Connections Inc.
Internal Communications Expert
www.StrategicConnections.com

Ian P. Buckingham

Founder & Owner of the employee engagement consultancy,
Bring Yourself 2 Work
Employee Engagement, Organization Development & Culture
Development Specialist
Author of *Brand Engagement: How Employees Make or Break Brands*
www.by2w.co.uk

Robert Morris

Independent Consultant for Accelerated Executive Development
Business Book Reviewer for *Amazon & Borders*
interllect@mindspring.com

Steve Roesler

Roesler Consulting Group/Steve Roesler Learning
Consultant to Executives
www.allthingsworkplace.com

Angela Maiers

Lifelong Learner & Literacy Coach
Maiers Educational Services
www.angelamaiers.com

PART FIVE

It's All About Lisa

❖

"As the mother of a 2 year-old son, I have already begun my study of the generation who will follow the Millennials. No names have been chosen yet for this new generation who will be starting college around 2018, but I do know that I'll be apart of the parental group who employers will either be thanking or condemning 20+ years from now."

Lisa Orrell, Millennial & Generations Relations
Expert, author of *this book*

CHAPTER SEVENTEEN

Specific Ways Lisa Can Benefit Your Company

❖

As I mentioned a few times in this book, companies of all sizes and in all industries contact me to consult with them on how to attract, recruit, manage, and retain Millennial talent and to help improve their internal *generation relations*. Although I do conduct a full-day business boot camp designed for the Millennial Professionals themselves, I spend a lot of my time educating HR execs and internal recruiters, as well as GenX and Boomer managers and executives, on the reality of this new (huge) workforce that is beginning to descend upon professional work environments across the U.S. and abroad.

Here is a current list of the keynotes, seminars, and workshops that I offer, but be sure to visit my website for the most current topics as they can change: www.TheOrrellGroup.com.

And, as my personal "thank you" for hiring me to speak at

your company or at your next event, I'll give you 10% off of my standard fees just for mentioning this book!

LISA'S SPEAKING TOPICS

SEMINARS

❖ **On-Boarding Millennial Talent: Insights and Strategies for Effectively Attracting, Recruiting & Retaining the Millennial Generation**
This is an in-depth 2-hour interactive presentation specifically created for HR, Diversity and Recruitment executives who want to improve their recruiting efforts for, and retention of, Millennial Talent.

❖ **Managing Millennials Seminar: How to Recruit, Manage, Motivate and Retain Our New (Unique!) Generation of Young Professionals**
The *Managing Millennials Seminar* is a 2-hour interactive presentation targeted at GenX and Boomer managers and executives to educate them about managing and retaining the newest generation to enter the professional workforce.

❖ **Global Millennials: Insights Into Our First Global Generation & Their Impact on Employers Worldwide**
The Global Millennials Seminar is an in-depth seminar that answers a variety of questions, such as: What other countries refer to them as Millennials? Are Millennials similar worldwide? Do other countries encounter the same management challenges that many U.S.-based companies do? Are other countries challenged with recruiting and retaining Millennial professionals? And if so, HOW are they handling these challenges? If your company is based

outside of the U.S., or if it is U.S.-based with offices abroad, you don't want to miss out on this valuable information!

❖ Millennial Sales Associate Acceleration Seminar

This unique presentation is for the new Millennial Sales Associates who have been hired by your company. You need them to be productive and effective quickly, and generating revenue for your company sooner rather than later!

❖ Communication Across the Generations Seminar

This info-packed presentation is for the multigenerational workforce that your company may be experiencing: Veterans, Boomers, Gen X and Millennials. We encourage all generations to attend the seminar together to improve relationship building and productivity as a team!

WORKSHOP

❖ Millennial Business Boot Camp

Ideal for the new generation of young professionals at YOUR Company! If your company employs Millennial Professionals ranging in age from 20 to 26, you need to contact Lisa for details about this one-of-a-kind workshop!

Her unique one-day program is designed specifically for the Millennial demographic and teaches them BEST PRACTICES IN: Business etiquette; leadership; management; communication; creative thinking; and more. This intensive boot camp covers everything they typically don't teach in high school or college...but should!

By investing in your new generation of employees, you're investing in your company's future! These young professionals now represent your company—*make sure they do it right.*

K E Y N O T E S

Lisa's keynote style is fast, fun and witty, with a concentration on
EDU-TAINMENT. Audiences come away with interesting insights
but find themselves entertained in the process. Her keynotes are
intended for business professionals of all levels, in any industry,
from all generations.

Currently, Lisa offers (4) keynote topics in the areas of Millennial
and Generation Relations. Each one is approximately 45 minutes
(can be shortened if needed).

For male & female audiences:
   1. Boob Tube versus YouTube: But Media Isn't The Only
   Thing That Separates the   Generations at Work
   2. Wired or Haywire: Are These Millennials Truly Special or
   Just Plain Nuts?
   3. Filling the Generation Gaps: But Are We Doing It with
   Quicksand or Concrete?

For women-only audiences:
   1. Millennials to Menopause: Can Four Generations of
   Powerful Women Co-Exist Without Casualties?

Lisa adds new topics regularly and partners with other experts to
create groundbreaking, highly educational and entertaining topics.
**For an up-dated list of her seminars, workshops, and keynotes,
go to: www.TheOrrellGroup.com or call Lisa at: 1-888-254-
LISA**

ABOUT THE AUTHOR

Lisa Orrell
Speaker ❖ Author ❖ Consultant

Lisa started her first advertising agency in Silicon Valley when she was just 25 years old and ran her award-winning company for two decades. And as a 20-year marketing and branding expert, Lisa has always kept her finger on the pulse of the "next big trends" that affect business.

Spotting the new *generation relations* trend several years ago, Lisa began researching the impact of the Millennials entering the workforce. This lead to writing and publishing the First Edition of her popular book: ***Millennials Incorporated: The Big Business of Recruiting, Managing and Retaining North America's New Generation of Young Professionals.***

Now, in the next phase of her professional life, Lisa has become a highly sought-after Millennial & Generation Relations Expert hired by companies, and professional associations, to educate their HR, Diversity, and Recruitment executives on attracting, recruiting and retaining Millennials. They also hire her to educate their Boomer and Gen X management teams on managing and retaining

Millennials, and on how to improve their *internal generation relations*. And Lisa conducts workshops for their Millennial new-hires on how to become effective members of their new work environments.

Lisa adds new content to her presentations and creates new topics regularly, and *her entertaining, humorous and informational keynote topics* are also getting attention.

Most recently, Lisa's media coverage includes (partial list): **Featured expert on MSNBC,** *Human Resource Executive* magazine, *HR World* (.com), *Diversity Business* magazine, *SMB-HR* magazine, *Recruitment & Retention* magazine, *Employee Benefit News, Pacific Business News, Black Enterprise Magazine, The San Jose Mercury News,* and *NewsDay New York.*

People also keep track of her unique insights and helpful tips by reading her popular blog, ***Lisa's Generation Relations Blog,*** at: Blog.GenerationRelations.com and by visiting her website at: www.TheOrrellGroup.com.

Contact Lisa today to consult with your company or to speak at your next event:

Lisa Orrell
Millennial & Generation Relations Expert
Speaker • Author • Consultant
Lisa@TheOrrellGroup.com
1-888-254-LISA
www.TheOrrellGroup.com
Lisa's Blog: http://Blog.GenerationRelations.com

❖

Printed in the United States
127240LV00002B/1/P